A Spiritual and Therapeutic
Guide to Peace

21 REFLECTIONS
FOR LIVING A
PURPOSEFUL
Life

ANDREA FORD

Dedication

To my mother, Gladys "Mrs. G" Robinson, and the loving
memory of my grandmother, Ruther "Madear" Bryant;
thank you for believing in me, loving me unconditionally,
and introducing me to God's love, grace, and mercy.

Foreword

Reverend William C. Proctor, Jr.

The author, Andrea Ford, has tenderly shared insights tempered by the whispered voice of God speaking into her soul. Her words are simple, not complex; uplifting, not fussy; but, instead, clear and comprehensible.

The timely contribution of this book adds to perfecting our understanding of how to live better among family, friends, and interacting with our community. It is soothing, fresh, lite, and ideal.

The approach is not "preachy" at all. Instead, one can receive the gentle but assuring encouragement to overcome our internal challenges. No doubt the author has written these words from the purest reaches of her heart.

Every message speaks with loving clarity. The messages focus the reader on how best to love, find love, and display love as children born of God. It is with honest pleasure that I commend the author and encourage each reader to receive these words of comfort, encouragement, and growth of our minds and spirits alike.

Table of Contents

Acknowledgments

First and foremost, I would like to give honor to God for giving me the vision, guidance, and discipline to write *21 Reflections for Living a Purposeful Life*. Thank you, Heavenly Father, for your grace to share your Word to those who have an ear to hear. May your Holy Spirit bless the hearts of men, women, and children across the four corners of the earth as we praise your holy name.

My sincerest thank you to Mitra Ramlogan, licensed professional counselor and certified professional counselor supervisor, who kindly provided the best spiritual and clinical insight along my journey. Since my moving to Georgia in 2013, Mitra has played a monumental part in my role as a therapist, a leader in the nonprofit sector, and in my biblical understanding of the Christian faith. I am grateful and deeply indebted to him for his brilliance, wisdom, and biblical teaching that influenced the overarching tone of *21 Reflections*.

A special thank you to Dr. Joel Floyd, author of *The Wait: Navigating Spiritually through COVID-19*, who helped me shape *21 Reflections* into a book with compassion and growth for readers. I am grateful for Dr. Floyd's knowledge and assistance in walking me through the intricate steps to publishing *21 Reflections*.

I would like to thank Dr. General Bryant, Jr. for over fifteen years of friendship and spiritual accountability. I am grateful for his pastoral guidance and biblical contribution to *21 Reflections*.

Thank you to my family, who has always been the backbone of my endeavors, and a very special thank you to my children, QuanTeric, Justice, Aurian, Artoinne, and Charity, for their love, patience, and support as I spent countless hours writing *21 Reflections*.

To my grandchildren, LaMyla Balcom and O'mari Graham, you are the newest generation of hope and inspiration. Through God's grace, you will continue His work of stewardship. May God's love guide you to fulfill your destiny.

Introduction

Many of us have experienced childhood traumas that have, for many years, resulted in a negative view of the world and oftentimes prompted unhealthy ways in which we interact with others. Some of us were raised in a culture by which we turn toward our faith for comfort and healing of our circumstances, while others, in search of instant relief, take on harmful behaviors such as using alcohol and/or drugs to cope with the thoughts and feelings related to their negative experiences. While there are a significant amount of people who seek professional help to deal with their issues, there remains a large number of people in society who have steered away from professional help due to a lack of trust or the stigma associated with seeking professional help. *21 Reflections for Living a Purposeful Life* is a book of hope and inspiration for people seeking a caring, nonjudgmental guide to healing. Moreover, *21 Reflections* offers a spiritually-based concept for embracing one's personal experience, while adopting the resolution and strength of Biblical principles as prototypes or a paradigm for our own healing. *21 Reflections* provides ensuing therapeutic approaches that challenge us to take a deeper look at who we really are and encourages us to maximize our God-given strengths and abilities.

As we journey through the next 21 days of reflecting on our life, accepting our past, and embracing who we are, let's remember that as human beings, it's OK to acknowledge our weaknesses and feelings or emotions that constitute our humanity. God does not expect us to suffer in silence nor overlook our human vulnerabilities. Contrary to the belief of many, confessing how we feel is not a reflection of our lack of faith, but rather a recognition that we need God to help us through our moments of despair. Let's be mindful that through our spiritual encounter with God, we can overcome our troubled heart, conquer our negative thoughts and feelings, and receive all the blessings that God has in store for us.

Day 1

COMPASSION KEEPS
US CONNECTED

As we interact with family and friends who are experiencing hardships, sometimes, our first response is questioning in judgment as to how their situation led to such an appalling dilemma.

When we assume this approach, we subconsciously lose our sense of empathy, sensitivity, and responsiveness. We become ambivalent and out of touch with their feelings and needs during their adversity. On the contrary, God desires for us to help our family, reaching out to them with love and compassion during their time of need. We can learn from Abraham in the book of Genesis that we must be compassionate and love our family through times of disappointment and despair. For instance, despite Lot's quarrelsome attitude toward his uncle Abraham before departing Canaan, Abraham was concerned about Lot's well-being after hearing of his trouble with an army of soldiers. Consequently, Abraham responded immediately to rescue his nephew from harm's way. We, too, can express compassion for our loved ones just as Abraham did. We can begin today by adjusting our attitude and tempering our impulses to socially and emotionally disconnect ourselves from the challenges that our loved ones experience. Furthermore, we can change our actions or inaction towards our loved ones by acknowledging our reservations, our apathy, and the root of our apprehension that causes us to be socially and emotionally aloof and detached from their reality. Then, we can gradually move towards restoring our spirit of compassion and regain the love and sensitivity needed to bring healing and restoration to our lives. Moreover, as we move toward reestablishing balance and equilibrium within our family, it presents us the opportunity to be vulnerable, transparent, and more self-aware of our limitations and ideology that prevents us from being a vessel of love and compassion most needed in the family.

Think of a past situation in which you allowed your judgment to inter-fere with helping a loved one during their time of need. Write the main reason why you withheld your support. Give one example of what you could have done differently. Example: Searched for a community agency that provides the support your loved one needed or displayed a more compassionate attitude in your tone of voice or demeanor.

Day 2

GROWING IN YOUR GIFTS

Each of us has God-given talents and abilities that we develop as we progress through life. As we experience daily challenges, we have an opportunity to fine-tune our gifts, strength, and endurance to sustain a new level of tests and trials. When we reflect upon the life of Jesus, Luke 2:52 affirms that Jesus grew in stature, wisdom, and favor with God and men. Likewise, we must continue to progress to achieve multidimensional growth, including physically, emotionally, socially, and spiritually. As we perfect our gifts and abilities, we must recognize that they come from God, and use them as tools and instruments in which we become vessels to honor what God wants us to be. We must be mindful of the refining process that we encounter in the analogy of the Potter and the clay, the goldsmith and the gold dust. God is the Potter, and we are the clay. God is the goldsmith, and we are the gold. For us to grow, we must subject ourselves to the Potter's hand, and for us to maximize the use of our gifts, talents, and abilities, we have to recognize that they come from God, and we must depend on Him for their development. We must remain connected to God as our source and continue in obedience and use our gifts for their intended use.

Identify two gifts that you possess. List two additional gifts that your friends and family members have acknowledged you possess. Write how you are using your gifts to accomplish your goal(s)?

_____
_____
_____
_____
_____
_____
_____
_____
_____
_____
_____
_____
_____
_____
_____
_____
_____
_____
_____
_____
_____
_____
_____
_____
_____
_____
_____
_____

Day 3

CELEBRATE YOUR VICTORIES

Celebrating achievements is an extraordinary time to express self-love and self-appreciation. There are many ways that we can enjoy our accomplishments, including having a pamper day at the spa, spending an hour or two at a golf course, or enjoying a quiet, intimate evening with our loved ones. Whatever activity that we choose, it should provide us with the feeling of joy, happiness, and a sense of accomplishment. The importance of celebrating our successes is to establish a positive pattern of owning our victories by giving ourselves permission to be proud and being bold to say, "I can do this, and I am enough!" Furthermore, celebrating our accomplishments gives us the intrinsic motivation and self-confidence to pursue and attain even greater endeavors. On the one hand, some of us have adopted passive behaviors toward expressing self-love and are often overshadowed with feelings of guilt for many reasons, including self-hatred or feelings of worthlessness. On the other hand, many of us do not want other people to misinterpret our celebrations as being proud and boastful. While Proverbs 27:1 cautions us not to be proud and boastful, there is a proper context in which we can be proud of our accomplishments. Furthermore, as we remain humble in our victories, we must also know that it's OK to embrace and celebrate every victory while knowing that God is the source of our achievements. Celebrating our accomplishments is a reminder that Christ is the one who strengthens us to be successful. We can repeat Philippians 4:13 by declaring, "I can do all things through Christ who strengthens me."

Identify a time in your life where you felt guilty for celebrating an accomplishment. What was your primary reason for not celebrating your success? What have you learned from that experience?

Day 4

BE FEARLESS

Fear is an emotion that serves to alarm us of potentially harmful situations. In this sense, fear is necessary. However, experiencing fear concerning our future and taking the first step toward achieving our goals are often triggered by our insecurities and feelings of inadequacy. When we allow worry and fear to overpower our lives, we give fear the force it needs to paralyze our inspiration and ambitions resulting in a delay of achieving our goals. To overcome our fears, however, we must question its presence by searching our heart: "Where does this fear come from?" While some studies suggest that we are born with some fears- the fear of falling and the fear of loud noise, many fears such as the fear of flying may be passed on from our family of origin. Similarly, we, too, can reinforce our fears and pass them down to our offspring. Therefore, we must be mindful that demonstrating fear through doubt, hesitation, or resistance toward setting life goals is being noted and modeled by our loved ones who admire and respect us. Furthermore, as members of our family, we can overcome the cycle of validating fear by substituting our use of fear-stricken words with more affirming and empowering words. 2

Timothy 1:7 reminds us that God has not given us a spirit of fear, but of power, love, and a sound mind. With the help of the Holy Spirit, we can conquer fear through our faith, courage, and tenacity. Additionally, we must ask God to give us strength and wisdom to face the root of our fears to grow more confidently in our gifts and achieve the purpose for which we were created.

List one fear that was passed down from your family of origin. How has your inherited fear hindered you or motivated you to accomplish your dream(s)? What fears are you exhibiting for younger generations to inherit?

_____

_____

_____

_____

_____

_____

_____

_____

_____

_____

_____

_____

_____

_____

_____

_____

_____

_____

_____

_____

_____

_____

_____

_____

_____

_____

_____

_____

Day 5

GOD IS YOUR SOURCE

What do we do during our darkest hour of despair? When no one is looking and no one is there to say, "It'll be all right?" The moment where we are faced with our raw, organic emotions that disturb our soul, how dow we respond? For many of us, our thoughts are consumed with the worst possible outcome that we lose our hope and deplete our last lingering thread of optimism. Sadly, this troubling state of consciousness is a dreadful reality that many of us experience over and over again. So, again, what do we do? How do we pull ourselves from this place? Unfortunately, some of us turn to behaviors and habits that numb our experience for only a moment. However, we need a lasting resolution that provides us with the hope to imagine a better and brighter version of ourselves and our future. God is the source of our existence and many of our experiences are directed and orchestrated by Him. Many of us have doubted that God is our Rescuer and Redeemer. Understandably, many of us take pride in being in total control of our situation and the outcomes that follow. Furthermore, we possess the need to produce concrete answers and experiences that give us the control that we believe we need in order to feel safe handling our issues. Besides, we do not want to sit back passively while waiting for God to show up. On the contrary, waiting as bystanders of our difficult experiences is not what God desires for us, and our getting to know God for ourselves will dismiss this belief. As we begin or grow our relationship with Christ, we will learn to appreciate and accept the fact that we cannot control nor manipulate God's timing nor plan. Furthermore, as our relationship strengthens with Christ, so does our understanding, trust, and faith in Him. Thus, we will learn to recognize God's wisdom to guide us to solutions that resolve our challenges, and in time, we will acquire or strengthen our spiritual discernment that warns us to avoid or disengage in behaviors that prevents us from recognizing God as our only source.

Reflect upon a challenging experience that you felt was your darkest hour. How did you make it through your experience? List two things you learned that can be used to help you during future challenges.

Day 6

HEALING IS NOT
ONE SIZE FITS ALL

Each of us, at some point, in our life will experience the loss of a loved one. It is a natural occurrence that often catches us off-guard. The current COVID-19 pandemic has claimed the lives of millions across the globe. The grief resulting from COVID-19 has been a global, melancholic experience that has left a lot of families feeling deprived of the closure that is essential to the healing journey. Furthermore, the manner of healing safely is a personal experience that takes time, patience, and permission. Grieving a loss is an important step that we must face during our healing process, and the way that we express our grief is often learned and emulated from our family of origin. Unfortunately, for some cultures, expressing grief can be uncomfortable and difficult to embrace. Many of us are expected to present ourselves as emotionless as we are faced with the cultural norm of being "strong." This notion can discourage us from being in touch with our true emotions, and as we experience incongruity with our emotions and expectations, it is very difficult for us to comfort and support others during their time of grief. 2 Corinthians 1:4 says that God comforts us in all our troubles so that we may comfort others in their trouble with the same comfort that we received from Him. Moreover, as comforters, we must stay in touch with our honest emotions. We must not guard our feelings against experiencing sadness, fear, or anxiety as they are fundamental to our being. When we become transparent and honest with our emotions, then we are able to become effective at exercising our ministry of healing by providing comfort to others in need.

If you have lost a loved one, list two healthy coping skills that you have used to help you get through your loss. Now, use your healthy coping skills to replace any harmful behaviors that you have adopted as a way of coping with your loss. Search the link below for support on coping with the loss of a loved one. https://www.apa.org/topics/grief.

Day 7

From Stone to Flesh

The presence of forgiveness is one of the earliest values that we have been taught by our parents, teachers, and other authority figures. The Bible mentions forgiveness over 100 times and declares that we are to forgive others seventy times seven. From a human standpoint, this measure of forgiveness seems highly impossible since most of us have difficulty forgiving one time much less seventy times seven. To be sincere in extending our forgiveness to others, we must know the significance of Christ demonstrating the epitome of forgiveness through His life and succeeding death on the cross. As we pray and work to transform the hardness of our heart from bitterness and resentment to love and compassion, we can demonstrate our forgiveness to others just as we received forgiveness from Christ. Many of us have to revisit the place that caused our pain, admit how we feel, and begin our journey of healing in order to change the way that we view life and interact with others. Ultimately, our forgiveness frees us from the bondage of guilt, shame, hurt, anger, and retaliation that we harbor towards others. If we demonstrate even a small measure of the compassion that Christ demonstrated for us, then our world will be a much better place.

Reflect upon an event (neglect, abandonment, abuse, etc.) that has resulted in your experiencing feelings of bitterness, anger, and/or resentment. Identify the underlying thoughts/feelings of your experience — hurt, worthlessness, guilt, and shame. Now use cognitive reframing by replacing the negative thoughts/feelings that you have identified with more positive thoughts/feelings. For example, negative thought: "I am worthless, and I deserved what happened to me." For example, positive thought: "My family and friends love me, and I am worthy and I was born with a purpose."

Day 8

TO HONOR AND DISGUISE

The Gospel of Matthew gives an account of Herod, the king of Egypt, who sent out his messengers to confirm Jesus' birth on the pretense of extending his honor. However, Herod was, in fact, planning Jesus' death as he was threatened by the Messiah's Kingdom. Herod's unsuccessful attempt to assassinate Jesus was blocked by the Most High, and Herod became even more determined to kill Jesus. While in a fit of rage and fury, Herod ordered the slaying of all the infant boys throughout Egypt with hopes of killing Jesus. After many unsuccessful attempts, Herod ultimately perished without completing his ill-fated plan to kill Jesus. The Gospel of Matthew can serve as a reminder that like Jesus, we were born with an assignment and purpose that threatens the evil work and plans of the enemy. As we look around in our society, we can see many subtle Herodian forces that disguise themselves as friends or supporters but have an ulterior motive to destroy our life's purpose, including the destiny of our family. We must become highly sensitive and aware of the evil presence that exists around us, and we must guard ourselves by petitioning God to give us the wisdom and discernment essential to protecting ourselves from the attack of destructive forces. Moreover, we can recite Psalms 91 to request God's protection and comfort during our times of trouble.

Identify your closest family and friends and write down at least one thing that each person has added to your life. If you are struggling to identify any value that your family/friends have added to your life, then it may be necessary to reevaluate their intimate access to your life.

Day 9

DIGGING DEEP

Jealousy is a strong emotion that we experience whenever we feel threatened by others. Jealousy is rooted in our feelings of insecurity and manifests to hatred, anger, and resentment while posing a threat to developing safe and healthy relationships. Although jealousy and envy are often used interchangeably, there is a difference between the two emotions. Envy is coveting or desiring another person's life, success or possessions, while jealousy holds intense feelings of bitterness or disgust. Regardless of the emotion we feel, God is not pleased with our ill feelings towards others and affirms in Proverbs 14:30 that envy is rottenness to the bones. Our feelings of envy and jealousy distract us from living out our purpose as we become too involved in the achievements of others while abandoning the opportunity to sharpen our own gifts. Furthermore, as we acknowledge and face the root of our jealousy, we can learn to value and appreciate our own abilities, qualities and personal successes that we have achieved. When we do this, we can counter any destructive feelings of inadequacy or self-doubt.

Reflect upon a situation where you noticed that feelings of jealousy were surfacing in your thoughts/feelings. Did you respond inwardly (I'm not good enough), or did you react outwardly (feelings of anger toward the other person)? Write three affirmation statements that you can use when you experience jealous feelings. For example, I am enough. I am beautiful. I am kind to others.

Day 10

WONDERFULLY MADE

Many of us feel troubled by our inability to defend ourselves and voice our opinion when we believe that we are being mistreated or taken for granted by people we love. Oftentimes, the decision to suppress our feelings and remain subjects of someone else's mistreatment or manipulation may be centered on underlying issues that we must face to end the damaging cycle of abuse. Studies have shown that approximately 85 percent of the population endure challenges of low self-esteem. To understand why a large amount of society faces issues with low-self-esteem, we must understand what constitutes our self-esteem. Self-esteem is merely the value that we place on ourselves or the measure of worth we attribute to ourselves, whether it's high or low. Furthermore, there are many factors that influence the level of our self-esteem. This includes childhood experiences or circumstances that transpire later on in life, such as abusive relationships, car accidents, job loss, and so on. Many of the challenges that we experience inadvertently impact our self-esteem by prompting us to doubt our abilities to perform tasks adequately. Unfortunately, the resulting low regard we hold for ourselves compounds over time as we neglect our mental/emotional well-being and continue in unhealthy relationships. Furthermore, as we continue to endure distressing situations, we adopt an unhealthy, inferior attitude towards ourselves. Ultimately, this leaves us vulnerable to other people's attacks or ulterior motives to take advantage of us during fragile life stages. To improve how we view ourselves, we can begin to revisit the experiences within our life that contributed to our feelings of low self-worth. As we gain insight into our negative way of thinking, we can begin to change our environment by demanding respect from our loved ones or removing ourselves from destructive relationships that affect our self-worth. We must also explore our God-given talents and abilities and appreciate them by giving them a high value and utilizing them to fulfill our purpose on earth. In addition, we must create a positive environment of people and activities that support building a healthy self-esteem. In doing this, we learn to value ourselves, demand that other people value us, and avoid people who continue to speak unkind words or display demeaning behaviors towards us.

Create a plan on how to improve your self-esteem. For example, use positive self-talk, establish boundaries with family/friends and learn to say no, accept compliments from others, compliment yourself, and speak assertively.

_____

_____

_____

_____

_____

_____

_____

_____

_____

_____

_____

_____

_____

_____

_____

_____

_____

_____

_____

_____

_____

_____

_____

_____

_____

Day 11

WHAT'S IN YOUR TOOLBOX?

Life happens! And when it does, we must explore every resource or coping skill that we possess to get through the trying times. As we experience hardships throughout life, we have an opportunity to gain valuable tools that we can use to overcome trials and tribulations that are certain to come our way. Furthermore, we must change our perspective on the way that we view our challenges. Instead of sighing dreadfully in despair at our circumstances, we can pray for God's strength and dig deep into our toolbox and use our faith, hope, tenacity, and courage to overcome our adversities. Having a toolbox reminds us that we are resilient. It empowers us to feel confident as we persevere through our hardships. Moreover, we must not waste an opportunity to use our tools. The current COVID-19 pandemic has forced us to open our toolbox and develop our creativity to adjust to a new way of living. We have an opportunity to sharpen our tools as we face the uncertainty of the pandemic. We can take inventory of our gifts and talents and explore ways to utilize them to persevere through our current challenges. Our toolbox of gifts and talents empowers us to face life with minimal stress and anxiety.

More importantly, as believers in Christ, our toolbox must be filled with the power of prayer. Our divine connection to Christ provides us with the lasting peace and comfort we need in the midst of all our encounters.

Make a list of tools that you are using during this COVID-19 pan-demic (e.g. going for a walk, writing affirmations, communicating with God more often). Feel free to add to this list as you develop additional coping skills and use them as needed.

Day 12

GOD'S GRACE IS SUFFICIENT

The presence of God is the most divine and awe-inspiring phenomenon that we can ever experience. Jeremiah 29:13 declares that we will find God when we seek Him with all of our heart. Seeking God, with all our heart, requires a commitment to putting Him first in our lives. This includes removing idols that we have been unknowingly worshiping: power, wealth, status quo, relationships, material possessions, and even television when it interferes with serving God. To experience the fullness of God, we must welcome Him into our life by studying his written word, praying and talking to Him daily to strengthen our relationship, and renewing our mind by replacing our negative thoughts with His Word. Moreover, the Most High is our Creator and knows us better than anyone else, including ourselves. He has the power to change the desires of our heart to assist us through our journey of serving Him and fulfilling our mission on earth. Jesus is our *peace, healer, and comforter* as we persevere through life's challenges. God loves us and cares about our experiences. He wants us to experience the fruit of His Spirit, including love, joy, peace, kindness, and so on. We must learn to trust Jesus and know that it is safe to take off the masks that camouflage our true selves, our sinful nature. God's love will cover us during our most vulnerable moments, and His grace is sufficient. We can decide at this very moment to accept Christ as our Savior, to dedicate our lives to Him through our worship and divine purpose. As we surrender to Christ, moment by moment, God will deposit His presence within us and give us the abundant life He promised in John10:10.

Let's have a moment of truth by listing two things in your life that may be considered an idol. These are actions, behaviors, and/or thoughts that have knowingly or unknowingly interfered with you putting God first. What steps will you take to remove distractions that are preventing you from getting intimate with God?

_____

_____

_____

_____

_____

_____

_____

_____

_____

_____

_____

_____

_____

_____

_____

_____

_____

_____

_____

_____

_____

_____

_____

_____

_____

_____

Day 13

IS THAT YOU AGAIN PRIDE

As we think about pride, we often imagine someone from our life who has an arrogant approach toward other people. This haughty attitude is not pleasing to God as it expresses that we are better and more important than other people. However, pride in this context is referring to our attitude that we can get through life without God. Being prideful in either capacity, towards our peers or with God, is sinful as Romans 12:3 affirms that we should not think more highly of ourselves than we ought to, but with sound judgment. Furthermore, God hates a prideful attitude that minimizes His Kingdom but places our trust in our own abilities, including our skills, knowledge, wit, and resources to fulfill our self-serving purpose. As Christians, we must discern that choosing the approach to operate within our own right is the sinful spirit of pride. For instance, King Nebuchadnezzar believed that he did not need God as a result of attaining power, land, and finances following his victorious battles with his enemies. King Nebuchadnezzar began taking on a prideful attitude that he was a god and desired to be worshipped as such. King Nebuchadnezzar was unaware that God permitted his victories to fulfill a divine purpose through his servant, Daniel. Moreover, despite God warning King Nebuchadnezzar to end his prideful attitude, to no avail, he continued in his sin. As a result of his pride and disobedience, God struck King Nebuchadnezzar with insanity, and he lived in the wilderness eating grass like an ox for seven years. Ultimately, King Nebuchadnezzar realized that his power was limited to God's permissive will. Consequently, he repented and transformed his pride to humility, and God restored King Nebuchadnezzar's sanity, honor, and his seat on the throne (Daniel 4:36). Like King Nebuchadnezzar, we must repent of our pride, acknowledge God as our source of greatness, and treat other people with respect and humility just as Christ commands.

When we fail to understand our prideful and arrogant attitude, it becomes difficult for us to see our true selves. It's common for us to have a blind spot that limits our ability to be honest that we are proud. Therefore, to gain better insight into your prideful ways, ask two trusted people to help you identify prideful or arrogant behaviors that you consistently demonstrate. The goal is not for you to feel attacked (which is rooted in pride) but instead to uncover underlying reasons for your pride (e.g. feeling inferior, low self-image, insecurity). Now, create a plan to transform your pride to humility.

Day 14

IDENTIFY YOUR DISTRACTIONS

Our daily experiences are saturated by various distractions that, oftentimes, aim to sidetrack us from achieving our goals. When we encounter situations in life that are centered on calamity, our first response should be praying for God's peace and discernment to respond appropriately. While it is tempting for many of us to respond in anger during negative interactions, we must always be mindful that we are fighting spiritual battles that seek to disturb our peace. We must stand firm in our belief that God will deliver us from the enemy and spiritual warfare that follow. As we encounter unpleasant spirits such strife, wickedness, and so on, we must discern their objective to incite mental chaos, which in turn distracts us from serving our purpose. However, through Christ, we can cast down the evil and wicked assignments and their strategy to deviate us from our destiny. Moreover, scripture warns us that weapons (distractions) will form against us but they will not prosper, and as we reflect upon the attacks on our life, we can affirm that the weapons that rose us against our peace, our destiny, and our life, did not prosper. We must reframe the way we approach our future by recognizing and removing distractions that are sent to destroy us. Furthermore, we can prepare ourselves by studying Ephesian 6:11, which affirms we must put on our whole armor of God so that we may withstand the wiles of the enemy.

Draw a pictorial image that represents you in the center. Then, draw arrows (assignments, distractions) aiming at you that evoke negative feelings, emotions, or thoughts. Next explore and plan how you can positively eliminate these experiences from your life. (For example, meditate twice a day for 30 days, replace negative thoughts with positive thoughts, take a 30-minute walk every day.)

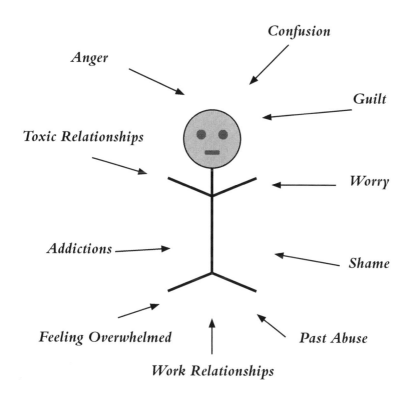

Use this blank page to draw an image of distractions that evoke negative thoughts/feelings/beliefs. Or skip the visual representation and write your distractions.

Day 15

CONTROL YOUR ANGER

During Moses's mission to lead the Israelites out of Egypt and into the Promised Land, the children of Israel complained to Moses about the lack of water. Moses fell before God in prayer to petition on behalf of the Israelites. Accordingly, God honored Moses's request to supply water to His people and instructed Moses to gather the congregation together and speak to the rock. Moses followed God's instruction of gathering the people together, but, instead of speaking to the rock, Moses struck the rock twice with his staff and water began to flow for the Israelites and their livestock. Moses's disobedience of striking the rock was not pleasing to God as he disregarded the opportunity to glorify God's name to the children of Israel. Consequently, God punished Moses for his actions by removing him as the leader to deliver the Israelites to the Promised Land. Like Moses, many of us have become frustrated with the assignment that God has given us to complete. Sometimes our frustration results from fear, lack of faith, or insecurity; however, as we experience hardship and obstacles in carrying out God's plan, we can pray and ask God to walk us through our reservations. Furthermore, while anger is a natural human emotion, God equipped us with an internal gauge that alerts us when our anger is increasing and on the verge of getting out of control and becoming sinful. Paul affirms in Ephesians 4:26–27 that we are allowed to become angry; however, we must not sin during our moments of frustration. Moreover, acting out our anger allows Satan to work against our destiny. We can learn from Moses's mistake by taking heed of our body's warning signs that protect us from losing control. Furthermore, paying attention to our instincts and impulsive reactions increase our insight and awareness into anger-provoking triggers and enables us to use good judgment during intense situations.

During anger, our body gives us warning signs such as sweaty palms, pacing back and forth, getting a headache, crying, and/or grinding our teeth, and so on. List the warning signals that your body gives to let you know that your anger is increasing. Now, state at least two things that you can do to avoid reacting impulsively out of anger.

_____
_____
_____
_____
_____
_____
_____
_____
_____
_____
_____
_____
_____
_____
_____
_____
_____
_____
_____
_____
_____
_____
_____
_____
_____
_____
_____

Day 16

Faith in the Fire

Faith is believing in God's Word without seeing any evidence that His Word will come to pass. Faith is essential to persevere through life's challenges, and growing in our faith allows us to trust God regardless of how the situation looks. Romans 12:12 reminds us to be joyful in hope, patient in affliction, and faithful in prayer. As we endure difficult life experiences, our faith is put to the test and we must remain grounded to resist impulsive urges to respond in panic. As we experience difficult challenges, we have an opportunity to demonstrate to people within our support circle that we are faithful and willing to trust God despite our circumstances. The book of Daniel provides us with a profound example of faith, dependence, and complete trust in God through the experience of Shadrach, Meshach, and Abednego. After refusing to bow down and worship King Nebuchadnezzar's god, the Hebrew boys were sentenced to death by being bound and thrown into a fiery furnace. As a result of King Nebuchadnezzar's extreme anger that the boys stood firm in their faith and trust in God, he ordered that the furnace's fire be increased with even more heat. However, while anticipating the horrific death of the three boys, King Nebuchadnezzar, in disbelief, witnessed the Hebrew boys walk out of the fiery furnace unharmed, unbound, and with a fourth man who King Nebuchadnezzar described as like the Son of God. Just as Shadrach, Meshach, and Abednego, we can exercise our faith in God and marvel at His glory when we are delivered from the hands of evil and prideful people who exist in our world today.

List two strengths (faith, courage, determination) that you observed from Shadrach, Meshach, and Abednego. Identify how you are using your list of strengths to honor God.

_____

_____

_____

_____

_____

_____

_____

_____

_____

_____

_____

_____

_____

_____

_____

_____

_____

_____

_____

_____

_____

_____

_____

_____

_____

_____

_____

_____

_____

Day 17

STICKS AND STONES

Many of us have quoted the old childhood saying: "Sticks and stones may break my bones but words will never hurt me." As we've matured into adulthood, we learned that the opposite is true: Words do hurt! In fact, many of us can recall the unkind words that were spoken to us during our childhood years and some of us continue to hold on to the pain of those words. As Christians, we should use words that edify and affirm other people, including speaking soft words to individuals who appear to have the spirit of Herod dwelling within them. Our desire to represent Christ through our compassion and kindheartedness must extend to people outside of our own spiritual beliefs. Furthermore, as we demonstrate the core of our belief, loving others, we can pay close attention to the convictions of our heart and resist impulsive urges to speak hurtful and sneering words that tear people down. In reality, the degrading words that we use toward other people are, ironically, a reflection of how we view ourselves, but, instead, we project our insecurity on to other people. Let's think for a moment – as we consider the human emotions: joy, anger, sadness, disgust and fear, a significant number of us, if we're honest with ourselves, can think of some mean or choice words that we have said or murmured to people who have offended us. All of us can use patronizing words to describe our frustration. However, we can consciously make a decision to use peaceful words that softens our anger as well as the anger of other people. Proverbs 18:21 tells us that life and death are in the power of the tongue- let's choose to use words that speak blessings over the life of others.

This is a tough exercise. Consider how your words impact your life and your loved ones' lives. Are they optimistic and hopeful or are they sarcastic, pessimistic, and judgmental? If applicable, reflect on the reasons why you use words to hurt or discourage others. For example, "To remain in control, Because I am unhappy with my life, I enjoy hurting other people." How do you plan to change your use of negative words?

_____

_____

_____

_____

_____

_____

_____

_____

_____

_____

_____

_____

_____

_____

_____

_____

_____

_____

_____

_____

_____

_____

_____

_____

_____

Day 18

RE-STORY YOUR STORY

Each of us has a story that we share with the world. We live out our story through our actions, inaction, words, and silence. Many of us have subconsciously created masks to conceal our stories from colleagues, friends, and even our own family. Our mask helps us to feel protected by safeguarding our hurt, pain, thoughts, and past experiences that we try to escape over and over again. On the contrary, our mask, to some degree, carries a sense of loneliness and emptiness. For many of us, it prolongs our inclination to become vulnerable and develop authentic, meaningful relationships where we can freely express the fears within our heart. Regardless of how bleak our experiences seem, there is hope for us to live a genuinely healthy life without the false sense of security our masks provide. We can accept our past and embrace our total being, including our perceived flaws and failures. Days 1–17 have prepared us for this moment – the opportunity to re-story our story. We have uncovered multiple layers of guilt, shame, bitterness, and so on, but more importantly, through God's grace, we have developed the spiritual sensitivity to acquire a greater sense of purpose for our life. Re-storying our story allows us to change the narrative of our past. We are not defined by the scars of our experiences, but they can serve as an example of how God will use our challenges to fulfill a greater purpose for our life. It is through Christ that we can re-tell our story as champions, and 1 Corinthians 2:9 tells us that God has a plan for our life that eyes have not seen and ears have not heard. This is a reminder that through Christ we can look forward to a future full of hope (Proverbs 23:18).

Day 19

GRATITUDE

Expressing gratitude for our health, family, and friends is essential to creating positive change within our life. It's an opportunity to view each part of life through a more grateful lens. Creating a gratitude jar is a great tool to use to express our appreciation for life. To get started on expressing our gratitude, we can write a statement of thankfulness at the end of each day, place it in a jar, and occasionally read our affirmations as a reminder that we have many things for which to be grateful.

Examples:

1. I am thankful for my family.
2. I appreciate my career.
3. I am grateful for my neighbor's kindness.

Search the link to learn more:
https://www.psychologytoday.com/us/basics/gratitude

Day 20

4-7-8

Utilizing relaxation techniques is essential as we reflect on past experiences. As we re-story our story, we can give ourselves permission to pause and acknowledge our emotions. Noticing our emotions is simply allowing ourselves to feel sad if we are feeling sad. Feeling our emotions, in this case sadness, allows for a genuine experience of being in touch with our reality, and while we are in our truth, we might have to take a break, relax, and use this 4-7-8 breathing exercise. We can practice our breathing techniques several times before we re-story our story. Let's choose life experiences that we can comfortably revisit and change the narrative.

Search the link below to begin this exercise:
https://www.drweil.com/videos-features/videos/breathing-exercises-4-7-8-breath/

Day 21

I Surrender

As we took on the tasks of evaluating our life, we were able to gain insight into the areas that have, for many years, been a blind spot that clouded our perception of who we really are. Many of us have hidden behind the mask of secular norms and expectations, thus, minimizing our life's purpose. However, it is time for us to give up our masks and allow God's grace to justify us through His glory and righteousness. This means that we can embrace who we are in Christ (without shame) and fulfill the predestined calling that we were chosen to complete. Furthermore, each of the exercises in *21 Reflections* was aimed at bringing awareness to our strength and resilience, exposure to our weaknesses to overcome our limitations, and more importantly, lead us into the fruitfulness and rewarding life of being in an intimate relationship with Christ.

As we grow in our relationship with Christ, we can appreciate that He is central to living a purposeful life. We can learn from King Solomon's experience that living a life without God is meaningless. Despite having wealth, wisdom, prosperity, and power, King

Solomon's life, in the end, was filled with spiritual depravity and despair. As we study King Solomon's experience in Ecclesiastes, we can discern that we will eventually meet face-to-face with our disobedience to God's Word. Nevertheless, we have time now to turn from our disobedience and embrace God's tugging on our heart and spirit. As God draws us to Him, we can let go of our guilt, shame, and condemnation. God loves us, and He declares to cast all our sins into the depths of the sea.

Moreover, as we dedicate or renew our life to Christ, let us pray that He will release us from our sin so that we can live a life of peace knowing that we are closer to God, and believing that we will receive God's gift of Salvation. Let us pray: "I firmly believe that Jesus is the Son of God, and He died for my sins. I believe that Jesus rose from the dead and sits at the right hand of God making intercession for me. I denounce the world and accept Christ as my Lord and Savior … Amen."

My hope is that God will enrich your life with His love and grace and bless you abundantly as you grow your relationship with Him. May you find peace and purpose as you practice the principles in this book.

Words To Remember

1. **Cognitive Reframing –** A therapeutic approach from cognitive therapy used to identify a situation or experience that we view as a problem. We alter our thinking to interpret the "problem" as a challenge and change our outlook to a more positive attitude to resolving the challenge.

2. **Re-Story –** A form of therapy where we focus on rewriting the old story of our life experiences to a more positive story that we embrace and live a healthier life.

3. **Coping skills –** Strategies that help us reduce and manage our reactions to stress-provoking experiences.

4. **Affirmations –** Positive statements that we use to dominate negative thoughts, feelings and beliefs about ourselves and our life.

Made in United States
Orlando, FL
13 May 2022

17801515R00048